BLAZERS

...den Worlds

BEHIND THE DOUBLE DOORS:
EXPLORING THE SECRETS OF A Hospital

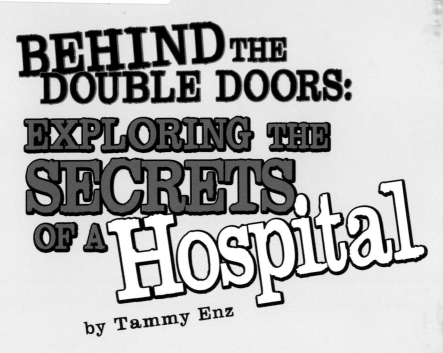

by Tammy Enz

Reading Consultant:
Barbara J. Fox
Reading Specialist
North Carolina State University

Content Consultant:
Daniel K. Zismer, PhD
Associate Professor and Director of Executive Studies Programs
School of Public Health, University of Minnesota
Minneapolis, Minnesota

CAPSTONE PRESS
a capstone imprint

Blazers is published by Capstone Press,
151 Good Counsel Drive, P.O. Box 669, Mankato, Minnesota 56002.
www.capstonepress.com

092009
005619WZS10

Books published by Capstone Press are manufactured with paper
containing at least 10 percent post-consumer waste.

Library of Congress Cataloging-in-Publication Data
Enz, Tammy.
    Behind the double doors : exploring the secrets of a hospital / by Tammy Enz.
    p. cm. — (Blazers: Hidden worlds)
    Summary: "Describes the behind-the-scenes places of a hospital" — Provided by publisher.
    Includes bibliographical references and index.
    ISBN 978-1-4296-3385-7 (library binding)
    1. Hospitals — Juvenile literature. I. Title. II. Series.
RA963.5.E59 2010
362.11 — dc22   2008054995

Editorial Credits
Jennifer Besel, editor; Bobbie Nuytten and Veronica Bianchini, designers;
    Eric Gohl, media researcher; Laura Manthe, production specialist

Photo Credits All images by Capstone Studio/Karon Dubke except:
Getty Images Inc./The Image Bank/Barros & Barros, 6 (inset)
Shutterstock/Andreas Bjerkeholt, throughout (concrete texture); Lagui, 9, 11,15, 21, 25 (paper
    with tape); Pokaz, throughout (grunge); Robyn Mackenzie, throughout (torn paper);
    Yurchyks, 20 (microscope)

TABLE OF CONTENTS

CHAPTER 1

AT THE END OF THE HALL

Doctors, nurses, and other
workers rush through the hospital.
They disappear down long hallways.
Where are they going?

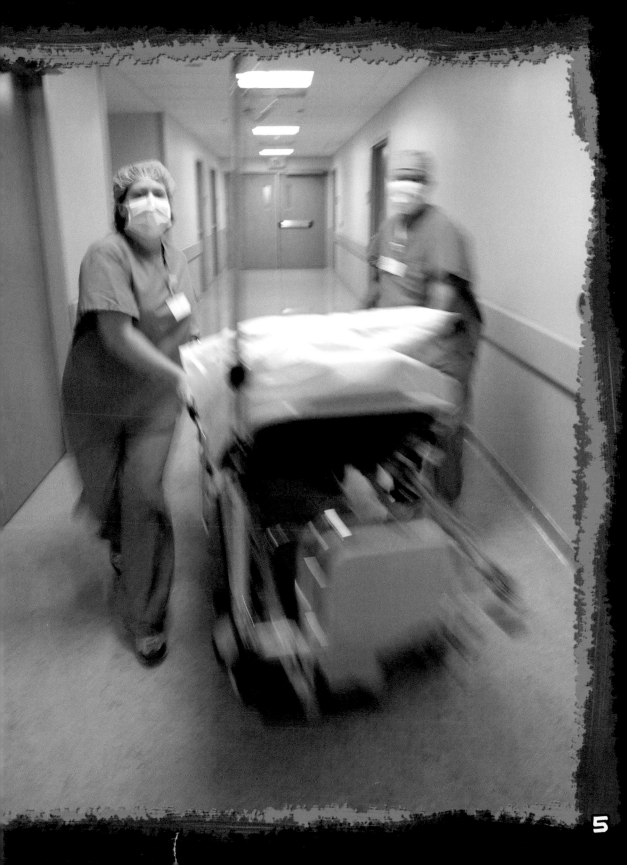

Down these long hallways, workers save lives. Hospital workers do their jobs behind closed doors. Their work has been hidden from visitors — until now.

CHAPTER 2

AUTHORIZED PERSONNEL ONLY

Sterilization Room

Visitors are never allowed in the **sterilization** room. This room must be free from germs so medical tools can be cleaned. Workers wear gloves, masks, and hair coverings.

sterilization — the process of making something free from germs

INSIDE INFO

Steam at over 250 degrees Fahrenheit (121 degrees Celsius) kills all the bacteria on medical tools.

MRI Room

The **MRI machine** is a huge magnet that takes pictures. It sucks in anything metal. Patients are searched for metal before entering the MRI room.

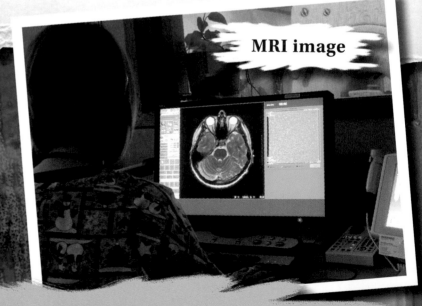

MRI image

MRI machine — a magnet that takes pictures of the inside of the body

INSIDE INFO

Patients with metal inside their bodies can't have an MRI. The machine's magnet would pull the metal out of the patients' bodies. The metal would tear right through their skin.

ID card reader

Locked Ward

Few visitors are allowed in the locked ward. People who might hurt themselves or others are cared for here. Workers must use an ID card to enter.

Cancer Center

Radiation beams are used to treat patients in the cancer center. These beams are harmful to healthy people. Lead and concrete walls protect hospital workers from the beams.

Radiation Oncology

radiation — the sending out of rays of light or heat

lead — a soft, gray metal

Workers go to another room while a patient is treated. They watch the patient through thick glass or with a camera.

Security Center

In the security center, workers control more than 100 cameras. They keep patients safe. The workers make sure no one steals medicine or equipment.

Security workers watch **restricted areas**. If someone without a pass enters these areas, alarms go off. Blinking lights flash on computer screens. The lights show workers which area has a problem.

STOP

NO UNAUTHORIZED PERSONNEL BEYOND THIS POINT

restricted area — a place that is only open to certain people

STOP
NO
UNAUTHORIZED
PERSONNEL
MAY ENTER

Laboratory

Hidden behind a locked door, lab **technicians** study blood and urine samples. They look at samples under microscopes.

technician — someone who does laboratory work

INSIDE INFO

Workers wear two pairs of gloves to prevent spreading disease. They take off one pair to scratch an itch or answer the phone.

Morgue

Dead bodies are kept cold in the **morgue**. Then they are moved out of the hospital. But you won't see bodies wheeled around. Workers use **freight elevators** to move bodies.

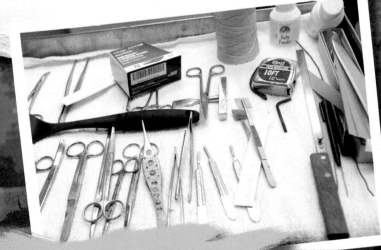

morgue — a place where dead bodies are kept

freight elevator — a large machine used to carry heavy loads

Air Handling Unit Rooms

Huge air handling units heat and cool the hospital. The units fill basement rooms. The units are so big that workers climb inside to fix them.

entrance to inside of unit

INSIDE INFO

Newer hospitals have sensors in the hospital rooms. The sensors tell the air handling unit to turn on only when someone is in a room.

HIDDEN HELPERS

For every hospital room you see,
there are many more you don't see.
Doctors and nurses use these rooms
to help people get better.

SURGERY — DO NOT ENTER

The next time you visit a hospital, keep a lookout. You might get a peek at the hidden world of the hospital.

Glossary

freight elevator (FRAYT EL-uh-vay-tur) — a large machine that carries heavy loads between different levels of a building

lead (LED) — a soft, gray metal

morgue (MORG) — a place where dead bodies are kept

MRI machine (M-R-I muh-SHEEN) — a magnet that takes pictures of the inside of the body; MRI stands for magnetic resonance imaging.

radiation (ray-dee-AY-shun) — the sending out of rays of light or heat; radiation is sometimes used to treat cancer.

restricted area (ri-STRIKT-ed AIR-ee-uh) — a place that is only open to certain people

sterilization (ster-uh-li-ZAY-shuhn) — the process of making something free from germs

technician (tek-NISH-uhn) — someone who works with specialized equipment or does laboratory work

READ MORE

Gordon, Sharon. *What's Inside a Hospital?* What's Inside? New York: Benchmark Books, 2004.

Murray, Julie. *Hospital.* That's Gross! A Look at Science. Edina, Minn.: Abdo, 2009.

Rosenberg, Pam. *Ugh! Icky, Sticky, Gross Stuff in the Hospital.* Icky, Sticky, Gross-Out Books. Mankato, Minn.: Child's World, 2008.

INTERNET SITES

FactHound offers a safe, fun way to find Internet sites related to this book. All of the sites on FactHound have been researched by our staff.

Here's all you do:

Visit *www.facthound.com*

FactHound will fetch the best sites for you!

INDEX